The Magic School Bus
PRESENTS
Polar Animals

Scholastic Inc.

Photos ©: Alamy Images: 16 top left (Masa UshiodaStephen Frink Collection), 22 top left (Steven Kazlowski); Corbis Images: 20 –21 (Frans Lanting), 3 bottom, 18 bottom right, 25 right (Momatiuk - Eastcott), 7 center, 28 top left (Paul Souders), 31 left (Wolfgang Kaehler); Dreamstime/Fotosutra: cover background; First Light/Mary Ellen McQuay: 16–17; Fotolia/Gentoo Multimedia: 1; Getty Images: 30 (Arnulf Husmo/The Image Bank), 8 top right (Daniel J Cox), 12 bottom right (Danita Delimont), 26 bottom (James R.D. Scott), 7 bottom left (Jim Brandenburg/Minden Pictures), 15 center left (Mark Hamblin), 23 (Mint Images - Frans Lanting), 11 center left, 11 bottom right (Paul Nicklen), 8 top left (Thorsten Milse), 15 bottom left (Wayne Lynch/All Canada Photos), 13 (Yves Adams); iStockphoto: 4 top left (DmitryND), 24 (RichLindie), 26 top left (twphotos); Media Bakery/Theo Allofs: cover; Minden Pictures/Tui De Roy: 22 bottom right; Nature Picture Library: 3 center, 14 (Andy Rouse), 17 bottom right (Chris Gomersall), 20 top left (David Tipling), 27 (Doc White), 18 top left (Edwin Giesbers), 10 (Franco Banfi), 15 bottom left (Jenny E. Ross), 28–29 (Ole Jorgen Liodden), 3 top, 6 (Radomir Jakubowski), 8 bottom right (Steven Kazlowski), 4–5 (Todd Mintz); Science Source/ Explorer: 31 right; Superstock, Inc.: 9 (Alaska Stock), 7 top right (Minden Pictures), 25 left (Norbert Wu/Science Faction), 12 top left, 19 (Wayne Lynch/All Canada Photos);

ISBN 978-0-545-68586-3

Produced by Potomac Global Media, LLC

All text, illustrations, and compilation © 2015 Scholastic Inc.
Based on The Magic School Bus series © Joanna Cole and Bruce Degen
Text by Cynthia O'Brien Illustrations by Carolyn Bracken
Consultant: Dr. Norman Ratcliffe, British Antarctic Survey

Published by Scholastic Inc., 557 Broadway, New York, NY 10012.

12 11 10 9 8 7 6 5 4 3   16 17 18 19/0

Cover design by Paul Banks
Interior design by Carol Farrar Norton
Photo research by Sharon Southren

Printed in the U.S.A.   40
First printing, January 2015

Contents

p. 6

p. 14

p. 18

At Home in the Cold

Ms. Frizzle told us to dress up warm. "We're going to the coldest places on Earth," she said, "the Arctic and the Antarctic." Polar bears and snowy owls live in the Arctic, while penguins live in the Antarctic. Seals and whales live at both poles.

In winter, the Arctic fox has white fur that helps camouflage it when it's hunting in snow.

B-R-R-R!

The Arctic is a cold ocean surrounded by land. The Antarctic is icy land surrounded by ocean!

Resting walruses
Frozen ice floats on the Arctic Ocean. Walruses rest there when they're not swimming.

Poles apart!

Where are the poles?
by Wanda

The poles are at opposite ends of the Earth. The area around the North Pole is called the Arctic. The South Pole is in Antarctica. The South Pole is colder than the North Pole. More mammal species live at the North Pole.

North Pole

South Pole

Feeding areas
Walruses choose sea ice that is close to shell beds in shallow waters, where they can feed.

Frizzle Fact
The Antarctic is cold but dry. It receives so little rainfall that it's considered one of Earth's deserts.

Arctic Life

Only the deep soil stays frozen in winter, so in summer plants can grow in the Arctic. When it snows, herbivores like the musk ox use their hooves and snouts to dig through to the plants.

Musk oxen

These animals live in herds of about 10 or 20. Their calves are very strong, and they can walk within hours of being born.

Musk oxen are herbivores. They eat plants such as sedge and willow.

The land at the Arctic is called the tundra—its deep soil stays frozen year-round. The animals that live here include the Arctic wolf and hare and the musk ox. They have developed ways of surviving the cold. Some animals, such as the caribou, live here in summer, but migrate in winter.

Caribou
The bigger a caribou's antlers, the greater its importance within the herd.

Arctic fox
This fox has brown fur in summer. It helps the fox hide among rocks when it's hunting.

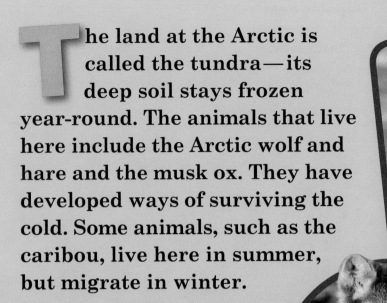

Arctic hare
This hare lives farther north than any other. Its extra-large feet make it easier to walk on the snow.

Survival skills.

How do animals live in the icy Arctic?
by Dorothy Ann

Many Arctic animals stay warm by growing thick fur. The musk ox has two layers of fur: an under layer that is short and warm, and an outer layer that is long and shaggy.

Other animals shelter from the cold in burrows. Foxes, voles, and lemmings dig burrows in the ground.

Finding food in winter is hard. Caribou have a good sense of smell and can find their food, lichen, even under snow.

Polar Bears

A polar bear's fur is not white, but clear.

O ne of the largest bears in the world is the polar bear. It lives on the Arctic ice. Polar bears have thick fur with a layer of fat underneath. The fat and fur help a bear survive in cold water. Polar bears are strong swimmers. They paddle with their webbed front paws.

A polar bear's fur has hollow hairs. These trap air and heat inside, keeping the bear warm.

In the fall, a mother bear builds a den to have cubs. The mother and cubs stay in the den until spring.

From the time they are around five years old, female polar bears can have cubs. They may have one to three cubs — usually two.

Frizzle Fact

Sunlight makes a polar bear's clear fur look white. Underneath the fur, the bear's skin is black.

Polar bear cubs stay with their mother for the first two or three years. She teaches them how to hunt.

That's a lot of food!

What do polar bears eat?
by Phoebe

If they're hungry, polar bears will eat all different kinds of foods, including most seals. But the bear's most common prey is the ringed seal. It finds the seals through holes in the ice called leads. Seals have a lot of blubber, or fat. Polar bears need this to build up the fat on their own bodies. A polar bear can eat 100 pounds (45 kilograms) of blubber in just one meal!

Under the Sea

Belugas talk to one another using clicks, whistles, and squeals.

Skin color
Belugas are brown or gray when they are born. By the time they turn five, they are white.

Frizzle Fact
Beluga whales have very flexible necks. They can turn their heads almost 90 degrees to the side.

The Arctic sea is full of life. Narwhals live there all year. So do beluga and bowhead whales. A thick layer of fat keeps these large sea creatures warm. Neither the bowhead nor the beluga has a fin on its back, and experts don't know why!

Point the way!

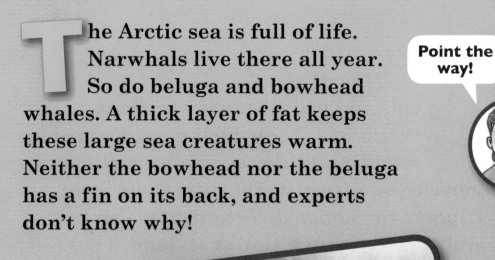

Why does a narwhal have a tusk?
by Ralphie

Narwhals have two teeth. In most females, these stay embedded in the jaw. In male narwhals, one tooth stays embedded, but the other grows through the lip. It looks like a spiral tusk, and it can grow to almost 9 feet (2.7 meters) long. Some females have a small tusk. In rare cases, a male may have two. Scientists have discovered that the tusks are full of nerves. This may be so narwhals can sense changes around them, such as water temperature.

Bowheads can live to be more than 100 years old.

Bowhead whale
This whale has a large, powerful head. It can break through thick ice when it needs to come up for air.

Narwhal
In the winter, narwhals travel in groups. They dive deep under the sea for their food. Narwhals find fish and shrimp to eat near the seafloor.

Seals and Walruses

Seals and walruses are excellent swimmers. Their bodies are shaped for speed, and their strong back flippers move them forward. They use their front flippers to change direction. Seals and walruses are much slower on land. They rest on the ice, and have their babies there.

Harp seal
Baby harp seals have fluffy, yellowish fur. It turns white after a few days, and then silver-gray.

Bearded seal
This seal's name comes from its long whiskers. It lives alone in shallow water with areas of floating ice.

Frizzle Fact
Harp seals can dive almost 1,000 feet (300 meters) under the sea. They can stay underwater for about 15 minutes before coming up for air.

Walruses spend much of their lives in water. They "haul out," or move onto land, in very large groups. Male and female walruses form different herds.

Those whiskers look ticklish!

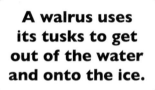

A walrus uses its tusks to get out of the water and onto the ice.

Why do walruses and seals have whiskers?
by Carlos

Whiskers are "feelers" filled with nerves. They attach to muscles in a seal's or walrus's snout. This means the animal can move its whiskers when it uses them.

Whiskers are very sensitive. They pick up movements in water. A seal can use its whiskers to tell the size and shape of a fish by feeling the trail the fish makes in the water. Walruses use their whiskers to help find food to eat in the dark ocean water.

Arctic Birds

Snowy owls ambush their prey.

The owl can attack almost silently. It has comblike feathers that muffle the sound of its wings flapping.

Snowy owl
The owl's excellent eyesight means it can see prey from far away. It swoops down to catch small rodents such as lemmings.

Adélie penguins live near the Antarctic coast. They dive into shallow water to find fish and tiny animals called krill to eat.

No way I'm diving in!

Expert swimmers
by Arnold

A penguin's wings are called flippers. The birds flap these strong, thick paddles to swim quickly, while using their feet and tails to steer. The penguin makes oil in its body. This covers the bird's feathers and makes them flat and waterproof.

Penguins can't breathe underwater. As they swim, they leap out of the water. This way, they can breathe in air and keep moving forward.

Family Life

Chicks stay warm in a parent's brood pouch. Mothers and fathers take turns looking after their chicks.

Emperor penguins live all around the icy coast of Antarctica. Male and female pairs gather in colonies when they're ready to lay eggs. Then the mother spends the winter at sea, while the father looks after the egg. He balances it on his feet to keep it off the ice. The mother returns when the chick hatches. She gives it food she's found at sea.

Each emperor penguin knows the sound of its chick's call.

My scarf keeps me warm.

Most emperor penguins live on sea ice. They gather in colonies in winter, when the ice is thick.

Penguins shed their feathers once a year, usually after breeding.

Group hug!

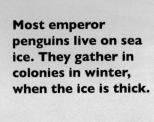

Penguin colonies
by Tim

Emperor penguins live in colonies of hundreds or thousands of birds. When it's very cold, they huddle together. The penguins take turns being on the outside of the group. Emperor penguins babysit one another's chicks in groups called crèches. The chicks grow quickly. By the time they're six or seven months old, they have their adult feathers. Then they are ready to go into the water to find their own food.

Frizzle Fact
The emperor penguin is the largest and heaviest of all penguins. It can dive deeper than any other bird.

Antarctic Birds

South Polar skuas build nests in high, open areas, where the winter snow clears fastest.

Penguins aren't the only birds that live in and around Antarctica. Other birds include skuas, petrels, and albatrosses. Most of these birds live around islands in the Antarctic Ocean. They feed on ocean fish and krill.

Snow petrels live near cold water and rest on icebergs and pack ice.

Snow petrels eat mainly fish.

Frizzle Fact

Male giant petrels are scavengers that feed on dead seals or whales. Most often, they eat animals that have died already — either during a fight or from starvation.

Black-browed albatrosses make their nests in large colonies on remote islands.

Spread those wings!

All about albatrosses
by Keesha

Albatrosses have the widest wingspan of all birds — the wings of the wandering albatross are about 11 feet (3.4 meters) from tip to tip. That's almost twice as long as an adult human is tall!

Albatrosses spend most of their time at sea. After hatching, a young albatross stays on land for up to ten months before leaving the colony. It will stay away from land for anything from five to fifteen years. It returns only to scout for a mate and somewhere to breed.

Antarctic Swimmers

Frizzle Fact

Many squid live around Antarctica. The Antarctic, or colossal, squid can be as long as 46 feet (14 meters).

Elephant seal

The southern elephant seal lives in Antarctica. It is the largest of all seals. It gets its name from its trunklike snout.

The Southern Ocean is icy cold. Some species of Antarctic fish have a special chemical in their bodies that stops them from freezing. Other sea creatures in the Southern Ocean include crabs, shrimp, octopus, and squid. Bigger animals—such as whales and seals—feed on them.

Gone fishing!

Krill

by Carlos

Millions of krill live in the ocean around Antarctica. Krill are tiny animals called zooplankton. Each one grows to about 2 inches (5 centimeters) long. A swarm of krill contains thousands of these tiny animals. Krill feed on phytoplankton, microscopic plants that grow near the surface and under sea ice.

Krill is important in the polar food web. Many sea creatures depend on krill as their main food. In fact, the word "krill" is Norwegian for "whale food."

Tentacles
Octopuses live deep under the surface. They use their long tentacles to catch crustaceans.

Baleen
A baleen plate hangs from a whale's jaw like a comb. The whale takes in water and strains its food through the baleen.

Baleen is made of keratin. Humans have keratin in their fingernails and hair.

Ocean Giants

Orcas, or killer whales, are ocean predators. They are speedy swimmers that hunt fish, seals, and other whales.

The biggest sea animals are whales. Orcas, blue whales, and sperm whales spend time in the Antarctic. It's full of food that whales like to eat. Humpbacks and minke whales also feed here. In the past, people hunted whales for food and oil. Today, there are laws to protect whales.

Orcas live in groups called pods. They click, whistle, and squeal to communicate with one another.

Sperm whales dive deeper than 3,000 feet (915 meters) to feed on squid. They can hold their breath for as long as 90 minutes.

Blue whale
The blue whale is the largest animal ever to live on Earth. It's as long as three school buses.

Time to eat!

All about blue whales
by Phoebe

The blue whale grows to about 100 feet (30.5 meters) long and weighs about 300,000 pounds (136,000 kilograms). It feeds on the krill that swim in the seas around Antarctica. Grooves that run from the jaw to the belly allow the whale to enlarge its throat and take in more water when feeding. The whale then sifts the krill from the seawater using its baleen plate.

The whale's feeding season lasts six months. During that time, an adult eats about 40 million krill a day!

Melting Ice

Walruses dive from sea ice into shallow water to feed. As the sea ice melts, walruses have fewer places to forage.

The world's climate is changing. Global temperatures are rising and the polar ice is slowly shrinking. It is getting thinner and breaking up. Animals like polar bears and seals are losing their habitats.

The Arctic is cold, but it's warming up.

The Arctic is warming twice as fast as the rest of the world.

Frizzle Fact

If all the ice at the poles melted, the sea would rise by more than 246 feet (75 meters).

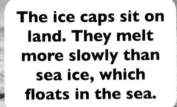

The ice caps sit on land. They melt more slowly than sea ice, which floats in the sea.

Protect the poles!

Endangered polar animals
by Ralphie

An endangered animal is an animal at risk of becoming extinct. Whaling caused the blue whale to become endangered. It is now threatened by climate change. Big fishing ships also hurt whales in the sea.

Polar bears are endangered, too. They hunt from sea ice when the sea is frozen. The food they find provides energy for summer months, when food is scarce. But the ice melts earlier each spring and freezes later each fall. Now polar bears must go longer without food.

Warming effect
Now that there is more open sea, the water takes in the Sun's heat and warms the planet.

Cooling effect
Sea ice reflects sunlight. This helps cool Earth.

29

Working at the Poles

Many of the people who work in polar regions are scientists. They usually work there in the summer months only, although some bases in the Arctic and Antarctic are occupied year-round. People must wear special clothes to work in these icy regions.

Oceanographers collect seawater to study. They take it back to science labs, where they can look at it more closely.

Oceanographer

The ocean is an important part of the Arctic and Antarctic. It affects the world's climate. Animals and other sea life depend on it. Oceanographers often study special parts of the sea. For example, marine biologists study the animals and plants that live in the ocean. Marine physicists study waves and tides.

Zoologist

A scientist who studies animals is a zoologist. Zoologists in polar regions study polar bears, penguins, and other creatures. They watch how these animals behave in their natural habitats and how they vary from one species to the next. For example, a zoologist might measure the wingspan of an albatross to see how large they can grow. Zoologists also help protect endangered animals and their habitats.

Glaciologist

Glaciers are huge sheets of ice. Glaciologists are ice scientists. They study the way glaciers form and move. The Arctic and Antarctic regions are full of ice. Glaciologists spend time in both places. They collect ice samples and carry out experiments on them, to see how the regions might be changing.

Geologist

Geologists study Earth. The areas around the poles are full of surprises. For example, there are mountains and freshwater lakes buried beneath the ice in Antarctica. Changes in landscape affect the way that the ice moves above it. Geologists work with glaciologists to study the effects of climate change.

Words to Know

Ambush To attack from a hiding place.

Camouflage Colors or patterns that help an animal blend with its surroundings.

Climate The weather typical of a place over a long period of time.

Colony A group of animals that lives together.

Desert A dry area where hardly any plants grow because there is so little rain.

Equator An imaginary line around the middle of the Earth that is an equal distance from the North and South Poles.

Extinct When a kind of plant or animal no longer exists, it is extinct.

Food web The complex network of related food chains within an ecosystem.

Habitat The place where an animal usually lives.

Hemisphere One half of a round object, especially Earth.

Herbivore An animal that feeds on plants.

Iceberg A large mass of ice that has broken off from a glacier and floats in the sea.

Lichen A flat, spongelike growth on rocks, walls, and trees. It consists of algae and fungi growing close together.

Mammal A warm-blooded animal that has hair or fur and gives birth to live babies. Female mammals produce milk to feed their young.

Migrate To move from one place to another.

Pack ice Sea ice formed into a mass when crushed together.

Phytoplankton Tiny plants that live on the surface of the sea.

Polar Near or having to do with the icy regions around the North or South Pole.

Predator An animal that hunts other animals for food.

Sea ice The thick ice made from seawater.

Species One of the groups into which animals and plants are divided by scientists. Members of the same species can mate and have offspring.

Tundra Arctic land that is frozen year-round.

Zooplankton Tiny animals that float in the ocean.